Dancing in the Alley
Poems for All Ages

Donna A. Monday

authorHOUSE

AuthorHouse™
1663 Liberty Drive
Bloomington, IN 47403
www.authorhouse.com
Phone: 1-800-839-8640

© *2010 Donna A. Monday. All rights reserved.*

Cover painting by Mary Gillim

No part of this book may be reproduced, stored in a retrieval system, or transmitted by any means without the written permission of the author.

First published by AuthorHouse   11/12/2010

ISBN: 978-1-4520-7433-7 (sc)
ISBN: 978-1-4520-7434-4 (hc)

Library of Congress Control Number: 2010913957

Printed in the United States of America

This book is printed on acid-free paper.

Because of the dynamic nature of the Internet, any Web addresses or links contained in this book may have changed since publication and may no longer be valid. The views expressed in this work are solely those of the author and do not necessarily reflect the views of the publisher, and the publisher hereby disclaims any responsibility for them.

Dedication

THIS BOOK IS DEDICATED TO my family, Charlie and Robbin Edwards, Zoe, Burk, Claire, and Gabe and to Dan and April Sellers, Avery and Katie. It is also dedicated to all other families everywhere, as families are the heart of love.

About the Author

Donna Monday is a former teacher who is that rare combination poet/car saleswoman. She has been writing poetry since she was 12 and selling cars for 21 years.

Her love of poetry came early. She was inspired by two poets, her father, Ephraim A. Arnold, and Hoosier Poet James Whitcomb Riley, both from Donna's hometown of Greenfield, IN.

"The first lie ever perpetrated upon me was that being a poet is the way to become rich and famous," she laughs. She's still waiting.

In January, however, she was named, "The Best Car Salesperson in the Village" by readers of the Zionsville Times Sentinel in Zionsville, IN. She edited that paper some thirty years ago.

"As editor of a small town weekly, I did it all," she says, "reporting, photography, police beat, sports, ad sales, everything. We had one murder case, and I walked into the courtroom knowing the judge, the prosecutor, the defense attorney, and the defendant The only person I didn't know was the victim."

Her most popular endeavor was a humor column entitled "Monday Madness," about the trials of motherhood in the village of Zionsville.

She penned the town's motto, "Zionsville-for a Visit or a Lifetime," which found its way unto signs, tee shirts, police cars and stationery for a quarter of a century. She was awarded the "Town Crier" Award by the Greater Zionsville Chamber and in 1986 was included in "Who's Who of American Women."

She holds a B.A. Degree from Hanover College with graduate work at Indiana Wesleyan and Butler University. She is "Grandma" to six beautiful grandchildren.

Remembrance

This poem was written by the poet when she was 12 years old and was published in the Greenfield Daily Reporter in Greenfield, IN. Her father, Ephraim A. Arnold, carried a dog-eared copy in his wallet.

A Child's Grace
For the robin in the tree
With her loved ones by her side.
For life and liberty,
The ocean with its tide.

The sun that greets the newborn day,
The moon that greets the night,
The Heaven that's so far away,
The stars that shine so bright.

For the snow that comes in winter,
For the birds that come in spring,
We praise you, God, with all our love,
And thanks for everything.

Table of Contents

English Lesson, Middle School	1
Melon Moon	3
Words Linger	5
June	6
Home	7
Heaven	9
While You Were Out	11
Grandma Was a Gemini	12
Widow's Song	15
Survival	17
Autumn	19
Words	21
On Becoming Forty	23
On Making	25
When I Found You	27
Coming Down	28
Reaching	29
Broken Promises	31
City Lights	33
Do It	35
Innocents Aflame, 9/11/01	36
Too Quickly	37
Sparingly	39
Why Not?	41
Beware	42
Believing in Spring	43
Empty	45
Finders Keepers	46
Ode to a Traveling Husband	49
You Asked About Spring	53
Giggles	55
I Once Knew a Place	57
Surprise	58
"My Birthday Suit"	59
Georgia Pines	61
Monster Love	62

Baby's First Haircut	63
In the Garden	64
Baby's Day	67
With Child	68
To a Newborn	68
Blow It	69
The Clown	70
The Turtle	71
Jennifer Johnson	72
Tommy Turtle	73
Playing	75
Noises	76
Puppy	77
Night	79
Sailing	81
Just You Wait	83
Air Mail to Santa Claus	84
I Wish I Was a Tiger	85
Ode to a Teddy Bear	86
Mustn't Do	87
April Grows Up	89

Photo Credits

Marie and Frank McGrath	2
J. Stephen Edwards	4
Marie and Frank McGrath	8
Donna A. Monday	10
Marie and Frank McGrath	16
Donna A. Monday	18
Donna A. Monday	20
Donna A. Monday	22
Donna A. Monday	24
Marie and Frank McGrath	30
Marie and Frank McGrath	32
Robbin Edwards	34
Donna A. Monday	38
Donna A. Monday	40
Marie and Frank McGrath	44
Robbin Edwards	48
Donna A. Monday	52
April and Dan Sellers	54
Marie and Frank McGrath	56
Marie and Frank McGrath	60
Jamie and Angie Ruch	66
Donna A. Monday	74
Marie and Frank McGrath	78
Donna A. Monday	80

Dancing in the Alley

English Lesson, Middle School

A little alliteration
Beats a lotta onomatopoeia

Melon Moon

A melon moon
You could eat with a spoon,
That's all there is tonight.

A lover's wish
On a crystal dish,
A curl of silver light.

A twist of "thank you,"
A slice of "please,"
In the midnight darkness glowing,
A rocking chair
Suspended in air,
With only the rocker showing.

A melon moon
You could eat with a spoon,
Served with a single star,
A lover's wish
On a crystal dish,
How beautiful you are.

Words Linger

I can't believe
A man's soul is truly dead
As long as someone, somewhere
Remembers something that he said.

June

God made for earth a night light.
He fashioned it of moon,
Then tossed a million fireflies
Below, and called it June.

Donna A. Monday

Home

Checks and stripes and polka dots
And flowers on the wall,
Bricks upon the fireplace
And mirrors in the hall.
Candles on the mantelpiece,
And pillows on the floor,
And definitely a welcome mat
And a wreath upon the door.

With doorbell chimes that really chime,
And floors that really creak,
Flowers all about the place,
And doors that sometimes squeak.
A porch swing is a must, of course,
As is a weather vane,
With a bedroom like an attic
That gets sleepy in the rain.

The bedspreads must be cheerful
And the windows let in light,
With lots and lots of rocking chairs
Out on the porch at night.
With dogwood, oak, and redbuds,
A ginkgo tree for fun--
Honeysuckle on the fence--
Tomatoes in the sun.
A lamp-post by the walkway,
And a morning glory vine,
With a rustic little mailbox
To tell the world it's mine.

Heaven

Heaven isn't really far.
It's just beyond the brightest star.
Hidden beneath the dark of night,
Heaven's just a hint of light.

It's just a glimmer--just a gleam--
Heaven's what you dare to dream.

While You Were Out

Spring came.
She was dressed in lace.
She smelled of lilacs,
And she washed her face.

Summer came.
She was dressed for play.
She smelled of sunshine,
But she couldn't stay.

Autumn came.
She was dressed in gold.
She smelled of apples
And complained of the cold.

Winter came.
She was dressed in white,
And poured herself
On me last night.

She's outside now, lying on the ground.
Says she'll wait 'til spring comes round,
Willing and eager to take her place,
Smelling of lilacs,
And dressed in lace.

Grandma Was a Gemini

Grandma Was a Gemini,
Though I'm sure she didn't know it.
Grandma was a Gemini,
Though I doubt she ever showed it.

She was also Cherokee
And beady-eyed,
And brave,
And tough as nails,
And worked like a slave.
Always did,
Cradle to grave.

Grandma was a Gemini,
A Cherokee Gemini,
A Bible-thumping
Cherokee Gemini,
Who knew poverty
And loss,
But loved large
And didn't count the cost.

Grandma was a Gemini,
Married a boy named Monday.
Loved him with a passion,
But couldn't keep him alive.
Diabetic coal miner,
He died at 35.

Donna A. Monday

Left her a Depression widow,
With nowhere to go,
Six children above ground,
One down below.

The two oldest married,
And off they went.
My mother and a sister
Were to an orphanage sent.

The two babies stayed with Grandma.
She hugged them, loved them, led them.
And God only knows
How on earth she fed them.
Grandma was a Gemini,
Sign of the twins, no less...

She told me once
At the breakfast table
She was always sorry
She was unable
To have twins.

"I had them named and everything,"
That day she said to me.
"Bertrude and Gertrude,
That's who they would be."

"I'd call them Bert and Gert for short,"
She said, a twinkle in her eye.
"But God wouldn't allow it.
I still don't know why."

The names Bert and Gert
Went through my mind.
I chose to say that,
"God is kind."

Grandma was a Gemini,
A Cherokee Gemini
With a secret plan.
She didn't teach it
Or preach it.
She just lived it.

Grandma's plan rarely missed.
And it went something like this.

Whatever hardships life imposes,
There are but two answers:
Love,
And roses.

Widow's Song

If I could be invisible
If I could pour the rain,
If I could sing the birds to sleep
And wake them up again--

Had I the wit of Shakespeare,
The beauty of Monroe,
The wisdom of Solomon,
The talent of Van Gogh--

I'd trade it all
For just a night
Of peaceful,
Dreamless sleep,
Cradled by your loving arms,
In silence, warm and deep.

I'd trade it all.
I'd say,
"Here, God,"
Thanks, but could you please,
Instead of all these lovely things,
Grant me only these:
"My husband's face
In the morning,
A child
Upon my knee,
A peaceful heart
At evening,
And a little dog who loves me."

Survival

In case no one
Has told you so,
All living things
Need love to grow.

Autumn

When I was young I liked spring best
Because I thought I should.
Spring was life and autumn death,
And life, of course, was good.

But now I'm older I can see
That autumn isn't
What it seemed to be.

It isn't death,
Not death at all,
Just nature undressing after the ball.

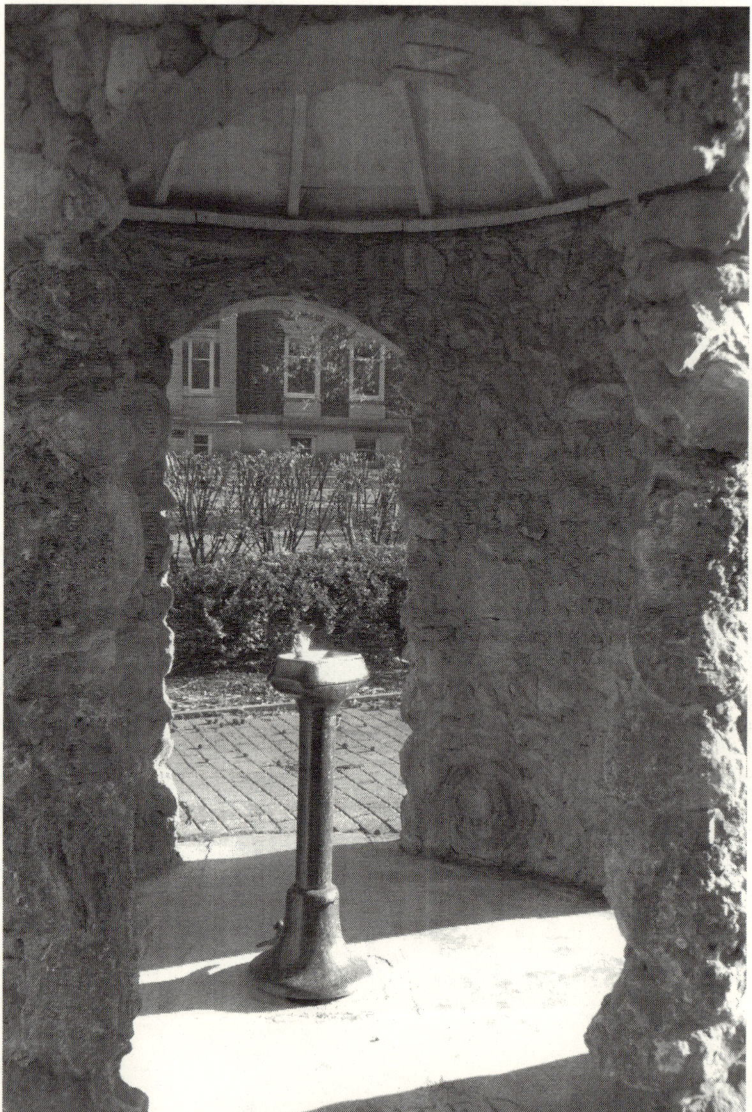

Words

Words are fickle--
Like a lover spurned,
Warm and cozy--
Then hurt and burned.

Words can be uttered,
Or muttered,
Or spit.
Words can caress.
Words can hit.

So, if ever I am impoverished,
Give me bread and give me drink.
Then, please, please, I beg of you,
Give me words that I may think.

Give me kind words,
Gentle words,
Words to soothe my soul.
Words to calm my spirit,
Words to make me whole.

For after the food is digested,
When the bread and drink are done,
The words will stay in my head like a song,
And they, like bread, will make me strong.

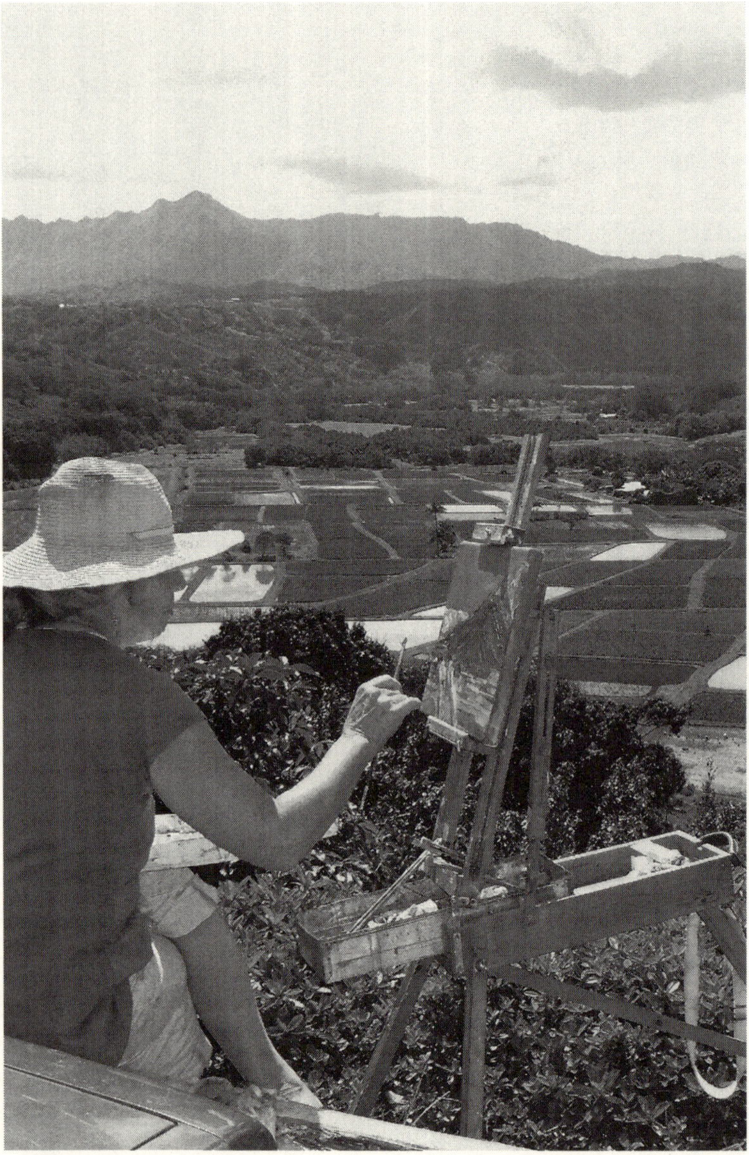

On Becoming Forty

I'm halfway done
Or only begun,
Depending on how you see it.

I've already been
What I'm going to be,
Or else I am learning to be it.

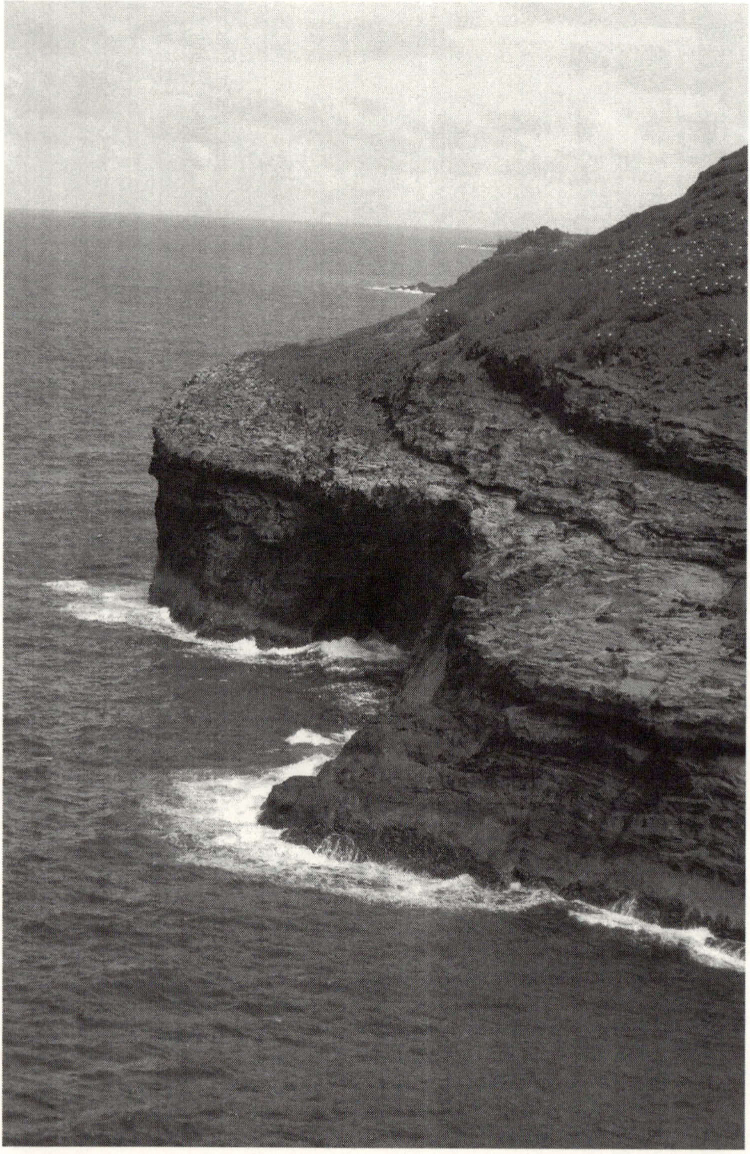

On Making

I have made promises,
And cookies,
And babies.
I have made yes's
And no's
And maybe's.

I have made mistakes,
And snowmen,
And a cherry pie.
I've made grown-ups giggle.
I've made children cry.

I have made memories,
And friends,
And birthday cakes.
I've made jack o' lanterns
And a few heartbreaks.

I have made gardens,
And prayers,
And bubbles.
I have made peace.
I have made troubles.

I have made wishes,
And money,
And time.
I've made people think.
I've made poems rhyme.

I have made music,
And dinner,
And tea.
I'm making a life.
Come share it with me.

When I Found You

When I found you
It was like finding a treasure under a leaf,
Gladness
After the grief,
And joy beyond belief,
When I found you.

When I found you
It was like finding the sunrise at the end of night,
Comfort
In the morning light,
And glory that it felt so right,
When I found you.

When I found you
It was like finding the moon reflected on the sea,
Ripples
Of eternity,
And wonder that it came to be,
When I found you.

Coming Down

Rain pours wet
With pity,
While snow falls soft
With grace.
And sleet comes down like punishment,
And slaps you in the face.

And love?

Love comes down like petals
In a fragrant summer breeze--
Uncaught,
Untamed,
Unbridled--
Elusive as the seas.

Reaching

It seems I've written
Reams and reams
Of dreams.
With a rainbow in my pocket
And an image in my brain,
Searching for the sunshine
While walking in the rain.
Climbing mountains
Going down,
Seeking farmers
In the midst of town.
Still...
I find them.
Walking backwards, yet gaining height,
As one must
When he wishes his kite
To soar,
Step back, and back,
And back still more.

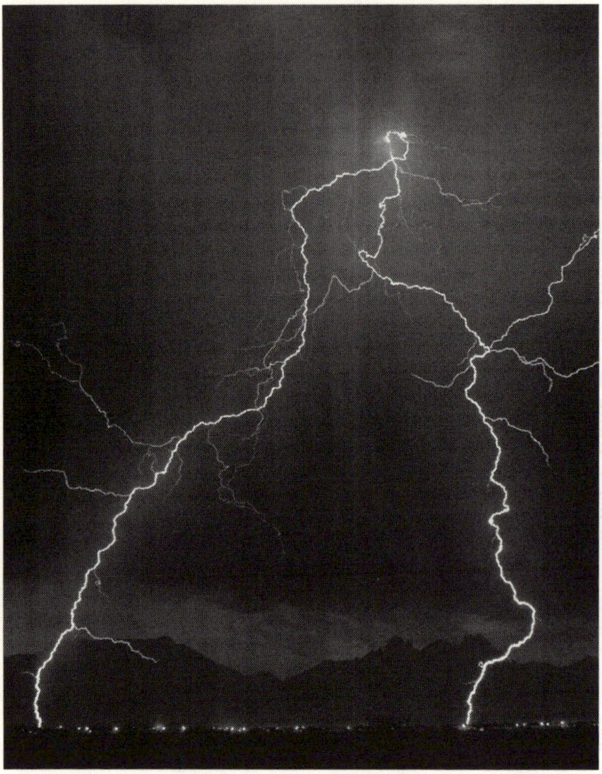

Broken Promises

They lie like shattered glass
Upon the bedroom floor,
Waiting, patiently waiting,
For someone to open the door
And step into the pain,
and then be gone again.

Hurting now, and bleeding,
Trembling in sorrow,
Shards of broken promises
Piercing their tomorrow.

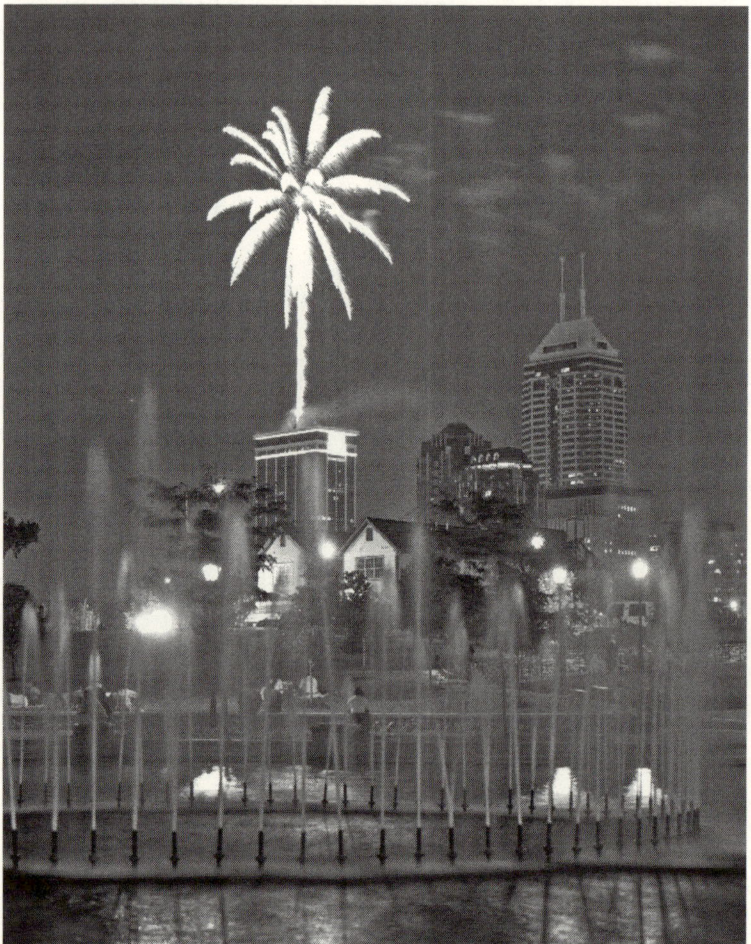

City Lights

City lights are brighter at nighter.

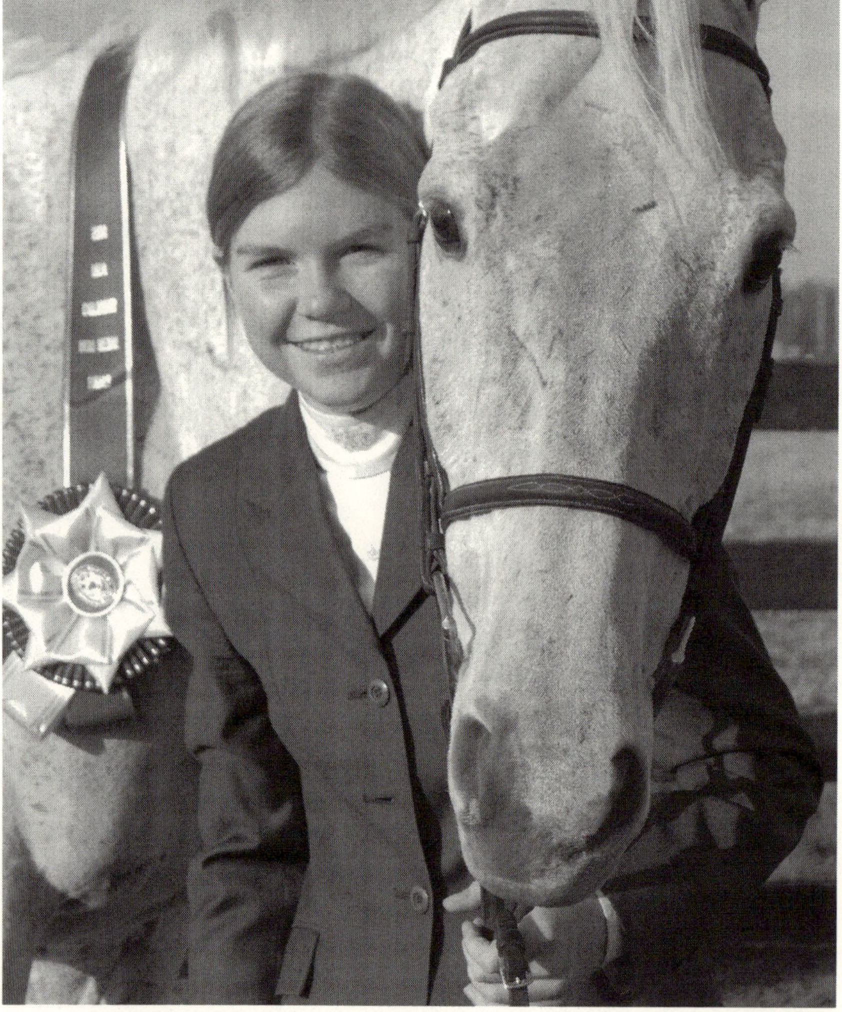

Do It

Anything you do
Is something you have done.
You cannot finish anything
You have not first begun.

Mistakes?
Go on and make them.
And risks?
Be sure and take them.

They're a little like the dark, you know,
Somewhat scary,
And then ,lo
And behold,
The stars come out,

And the night isn't scary at all.

Innocents Aflame, 9/11/01

You Satanic ship of fools,
With your cargo of cruel fuels--
Flaming innocents--
In the name of Allah hurled
At an unsuspecting world.

What mercy will God show you?
Will He profess to know you?
When you stand in sight of Paradise,
Expecting honor to your name,
Will He set you aflame
In the name of Allah,
And scorch the gates of Heaven?

Or will He prove to be
A god of irony?

Will He send you back to earth--
This time of humble birth--
A female born in Afghanistan
To members of the Taliban?

Donna A. Monday

Too Quickly

A baby playing in the sand,
An astronaut on the moon--
Both exploring an unknown land
They will have to leave too soon.

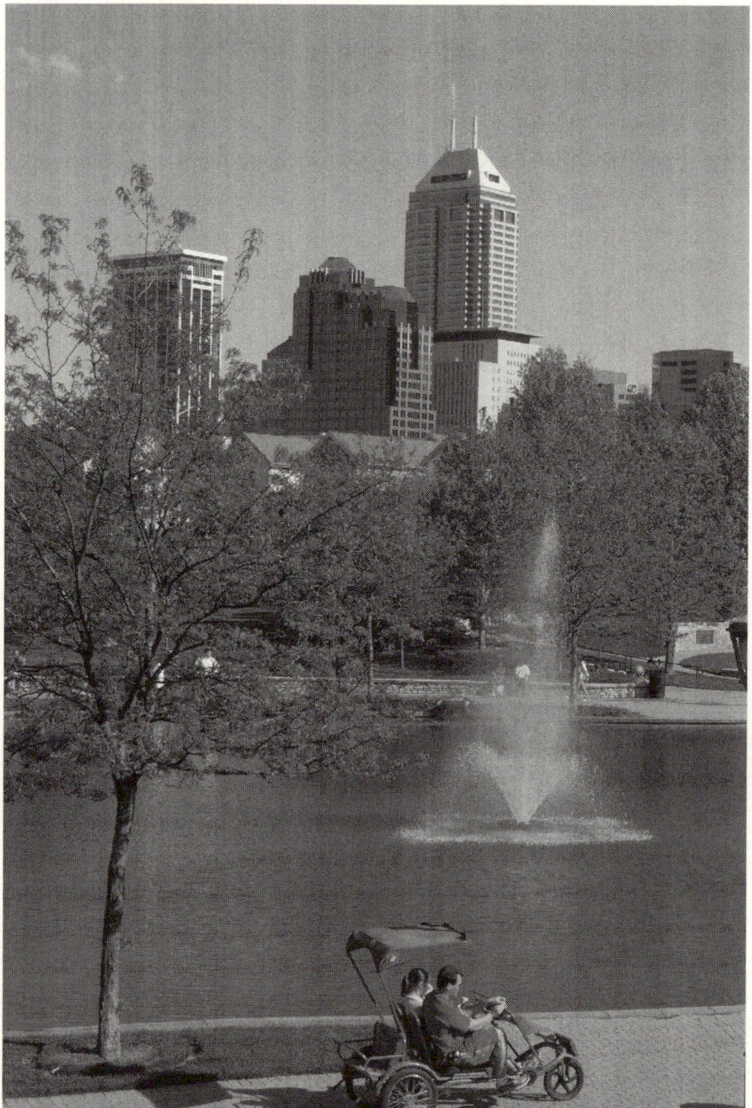

Sparingly

The sun to me is like prime filet.
I wouldn't want it every day.
I like it sparsely,
Now and then,
Gone awhile--
Then back again.

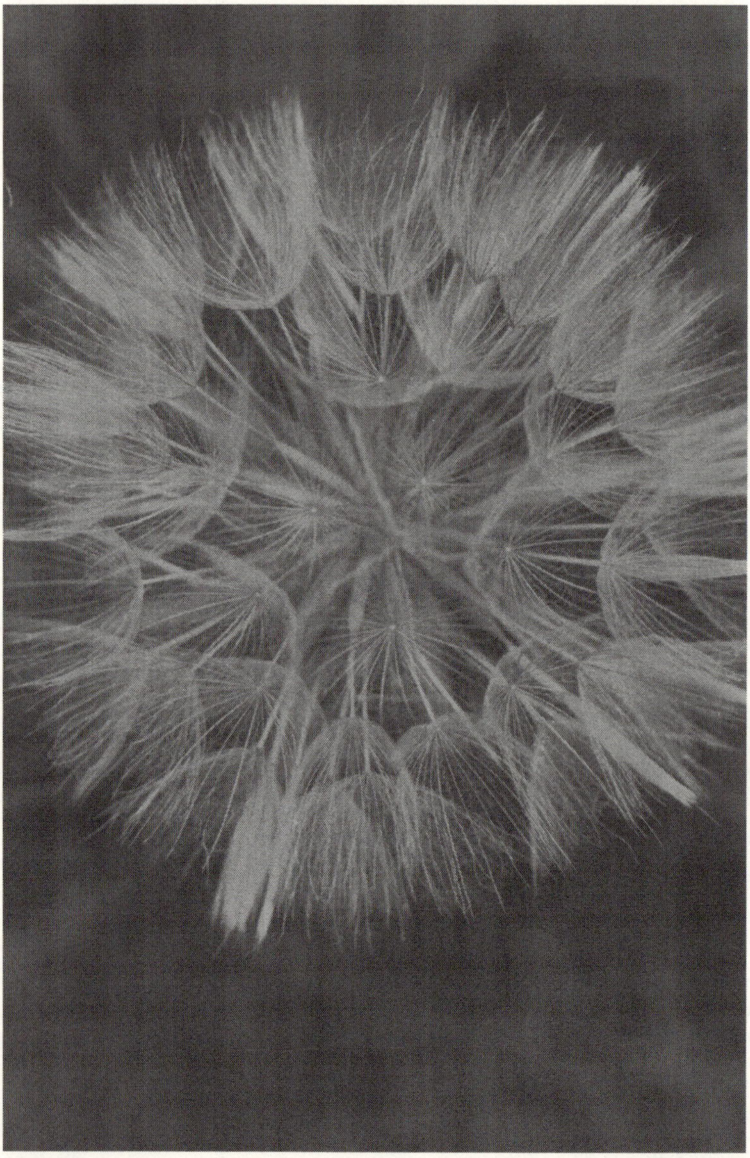

Why Not?

Why shouldn't a bride wear lace?
Spring does.

Beware

The hollyhock were talking to the roses in the alley,
The alley behind the house.
The morning glory vine crept up to listen in,
As quiet as a mouse.

"Did you see Johnny playing yesterday
When Jimmy grabbed his ball?
I watched the whole thing happen;
And it wasn't nice at all.

And then when Jimmy started home
He kicked Miss Sally's screen
And tore a hole and ran away.
He's the meanest child I've seen'"

"We couldn't agree more with you,"
Said the roses all at once.
"He's rude and crude and disgusting,
A bully and a dunce."

The morning glory vine
Crept silently from her place,
Pulled taut across the alley,
And tripped Jimmy on his face.

Now, in case you all are wondering,
What the moral of this story's;
If you're rude and crude and disgusting,
Stay away from morning glories.

Donna A. Monday

Believing in Spring

It's hard to believe
In the spring of the year
That there will be a fall.
It's hard to believe in winter
That spring was here at all.

It's hard to believe
When limbs stand bare
And naked in the breeze,
That God will turn them
Green again,
And give us back our trees.

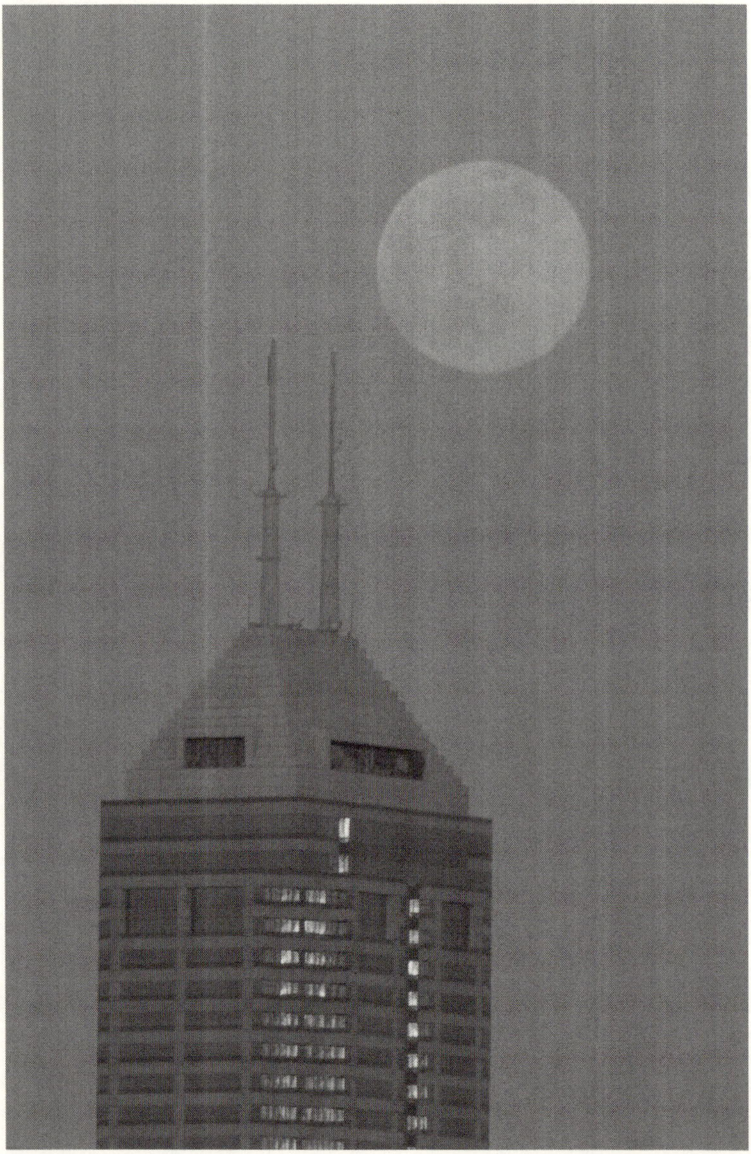

Empty

There are a million stars
In the sky tonight
And a hole where the moon should be.
And that walk we took--
Just you and I,
Is but a memory.

For a love unspoken
Is a love unclaimed,
And can never grow
If never named.
So, for lack of words
A love did die.

And I am left with a moonless sky,
And a hole where the moon should be.

Finders Keepers

Finders keepers
We used to say,
A form of cheating
That was only play.

But like all games
Of innocent youth,
Finders keepers
Has a grain of truth.

For among all people,
Both saints and sinners,
The finders who are keepers
Are those who are the winners.

For those who find a memory
And keep it through the years
Are those who store a thousand smiles
With which to meet life's tears.

And those who find a friendship
And keep it safe and snug,
Are those who reach for others
And find a waiting hug.

Those who find a rainbow
And keep its arc of hope
Are those who have within them
The ability to cope.

Donna A. Monday

And those who find a sunset
And keep its peaceful balm
Are those who at the close of day
Know where to find the calm.

It's always the feeling people,
The laughers and the weepers,
Who, when the game of life is done,
Are the finders who are keepers.

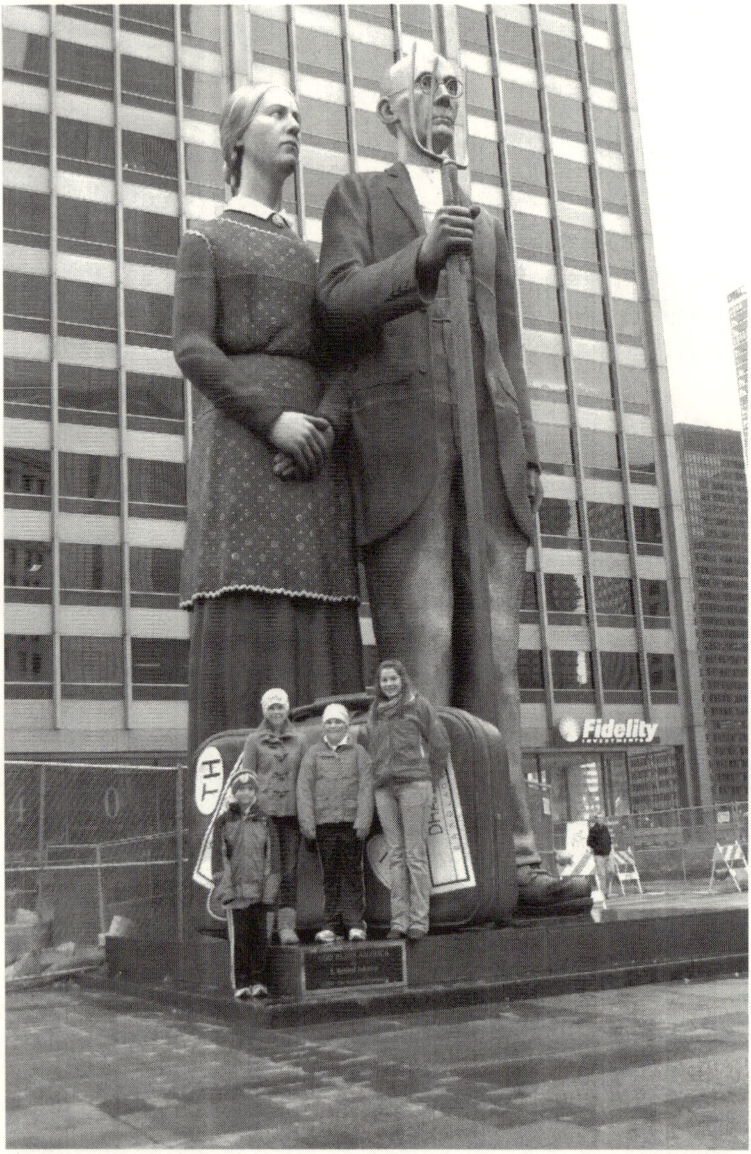
Fidelity

Ode to a Traveling Husband

He's taken out the road map.
He's washed and shined the car.
It's obvious we're going.
I wonder now, how far.

He's checking points of interest
And stops along the way,
And grins behind the atlas
With little else to say.

He speaks to me in numbers
And talks of miles per day.
He's told me we are going,
But where he will not say.

He's mentioned Arizona
And Salt Lake City, too.
But, then, he's also mentioned
The local city zoo.

He loves the painted desert.
He likes the rolling hills.
I wonder if he's thought about
The mounting motel bills.

But little does it matter,
The cost or the location.
He's made it very clear to me,
We're taking a vacation.

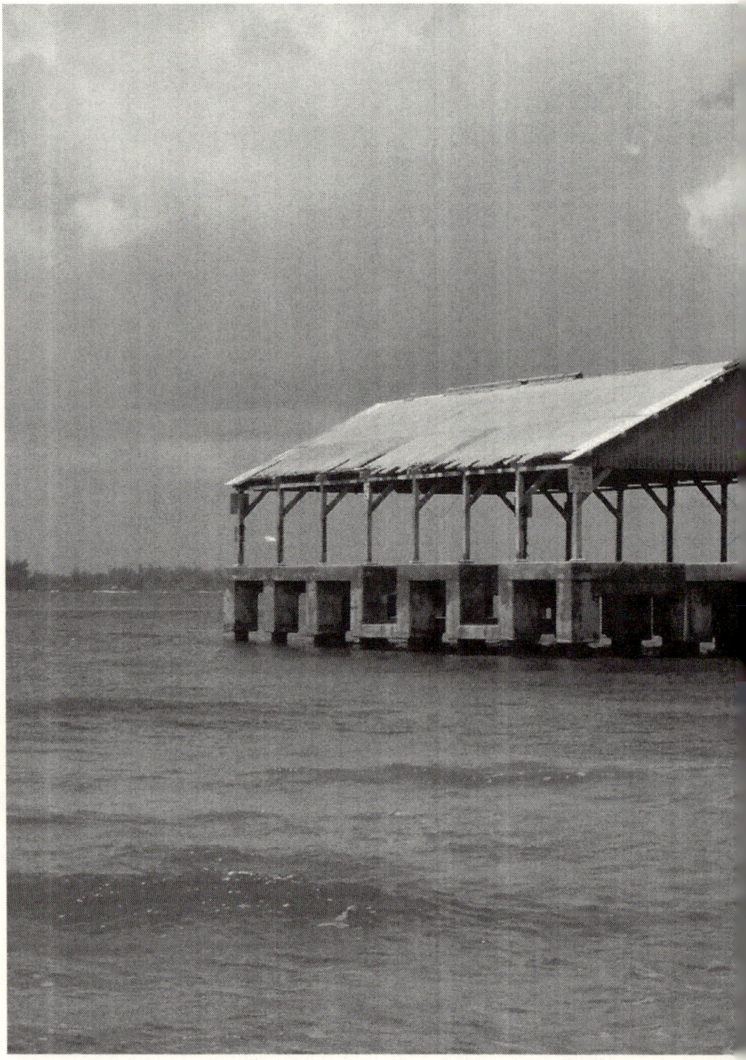

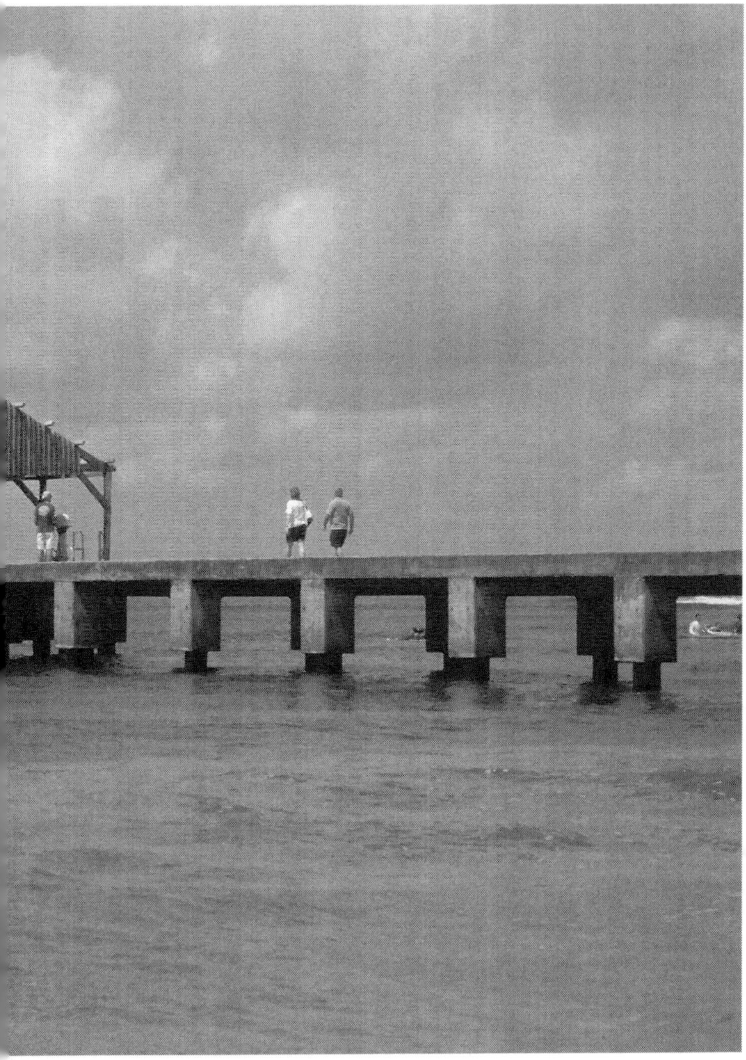

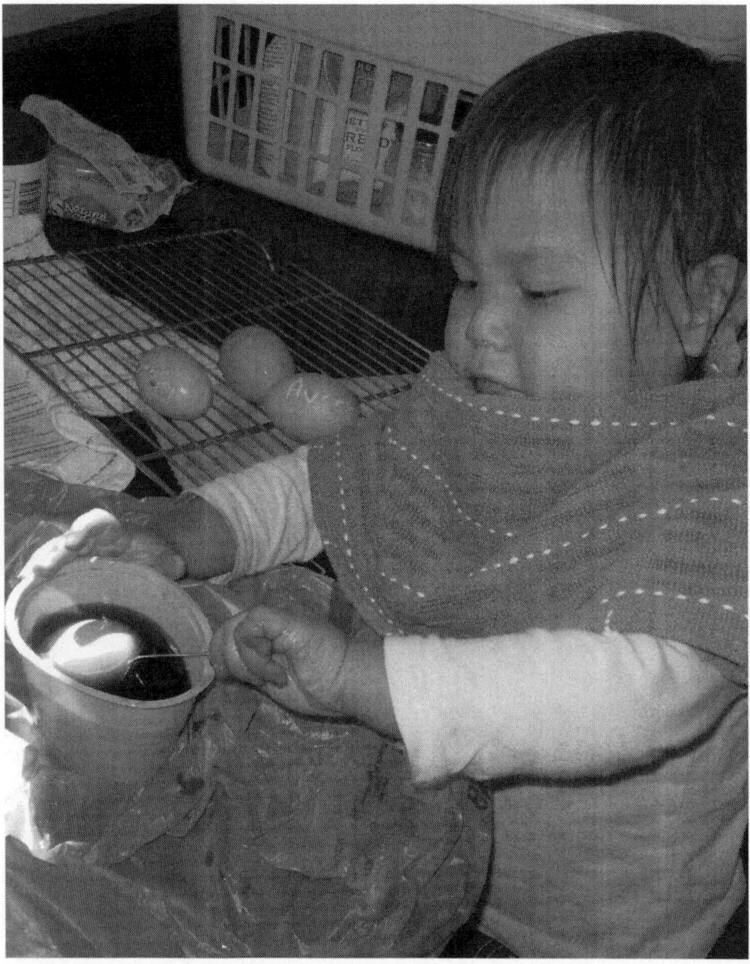

You Asked About Spring

Softly and gently a
Prayer in the wind
Rings out the world's message:
It's that time again.
Now breathe, Mother Earth, and ne'er be the same.
Green be your color, and Spring be your name.

And what is the Spring?
Why, listen my child.

Spring is the earth and the green of the earth,
The air and the smell of the air.
It's a sunny dandelion--a smile in the grass.
Spring is all this and a great deal more.
It's the dusty rose sunset,
The bright yellow dawn,
God's finger painting in the sky.
It's the softness of blossoms,
The strength of a storm,
A whispered memory of a season gone by.
Spring is a promise; spring is a date
With life for a moment in a world without hate.
A little boy's kite
Flown high in the air;
Spring is a kiss, a laugh, and a prayer.

This, my dearest, is spring.

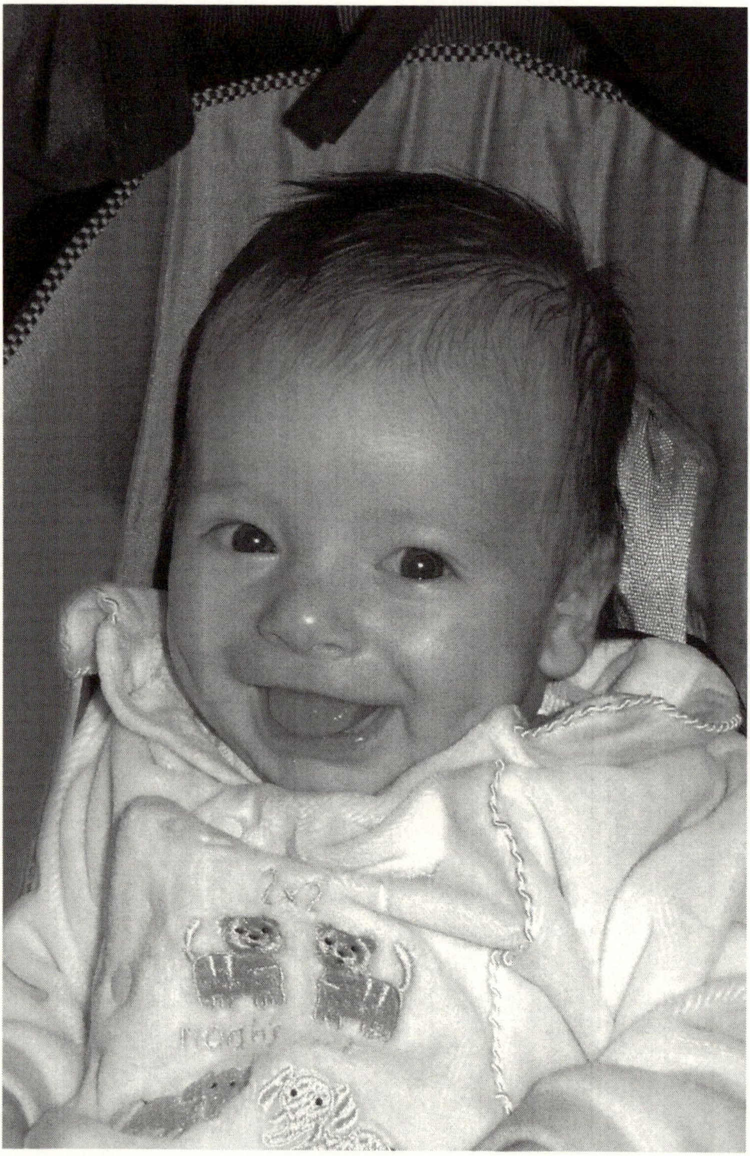

Giggles

Have you ever got the giggles
And giggled and giggled some more,
And giggled and giggled and giggled
Until your giggler got sore?

And when you'd finished giggling,
You took a breath and THEN,
Your friend came down with giggles,
And it started all over again.

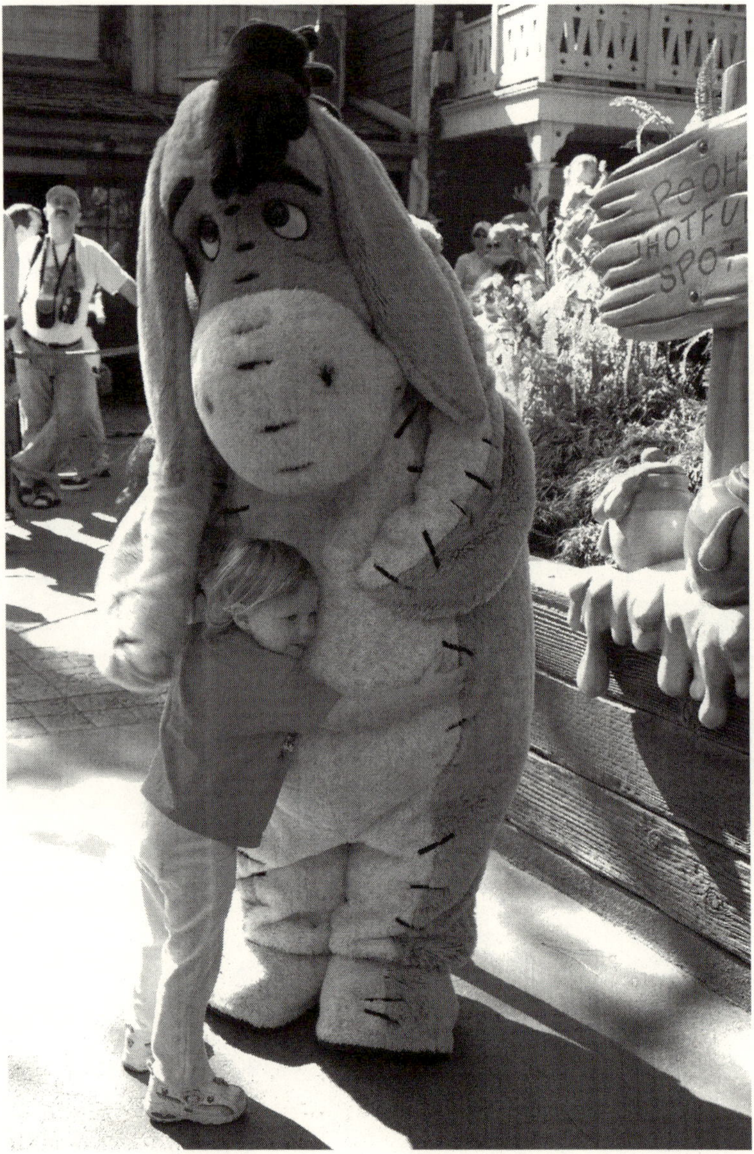

I Once Knew a Place

Where snowflakes were purple.
The trees all were red,
And an elephant slept
At the foot of my bed.

The queen wore her crown
On the tip of her nose.
Tigers had spots,
And lions wore clothes.

Clocks told the date,
Newspapers the time.
Cousins were free,
But friends cost a dime.

Puppies walked boys
And girls on a leash,
And instead of dessert
You were given a wish.

All the promises kept themselves.
The tooth fairy wore a hat.
And, when you are big, you can ask a pig
Where this magic place is at.

Surprise

While baby Charlie Edwards
Was upstairs fast asleep,
A little elf named Smiley
Did through the keyhole creep.

He hung upon the ceiling
A thousand silver stars
And left within the night drawer
A dozen chocolate bars.

A teddy bear named Henry
He left at Charlie's feet,
Then placed a wooden soldier
Upon the window seat.

He scattered on the carpet
A trail of pixie dust,
Then vanished through the keyhole,
As elves named Smiley must.

Donna A. Monday

"My Birthday Suit"
Grandma looks in the mirror

It's older and wrinkled
But still kind of cute.
I'd like to thank Mama
For my birthday suit.

It was quite petite
The way she sized it,
But to tell the truth,
I've really prized it.

I've come to love it,
This suit of mine.
Yep, my birthday suit
Just suits me fine.

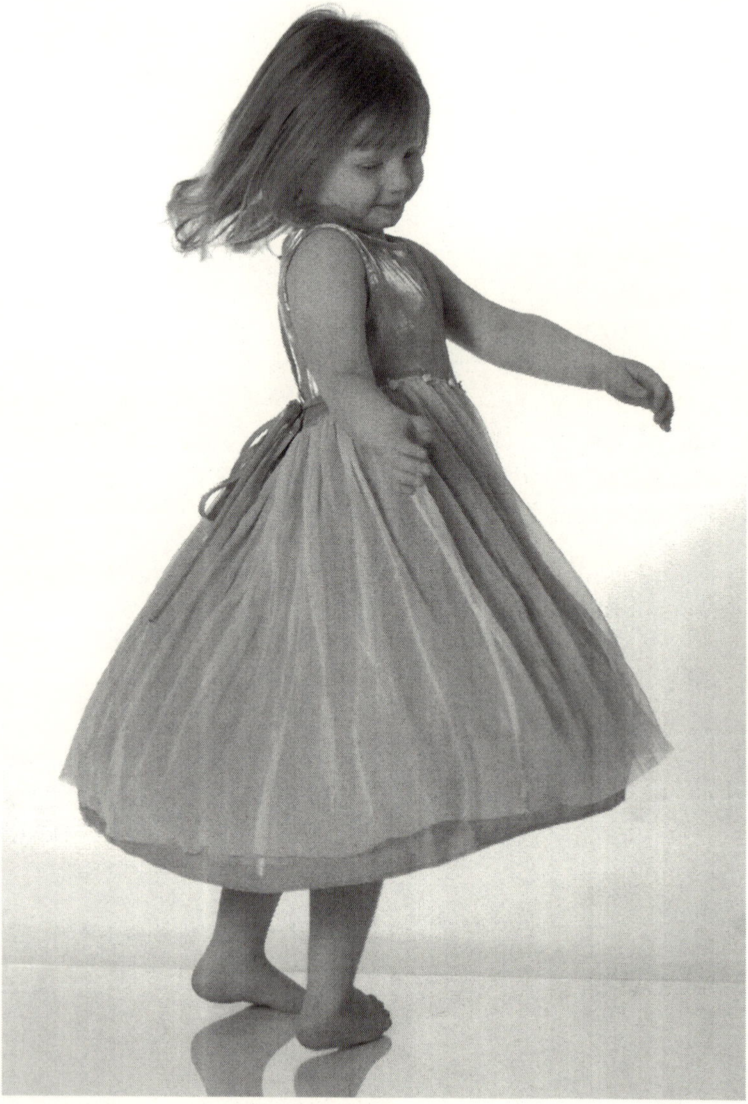

Georgia Pines

The Georgia pines are swaying,
The Georgia pines are playing.
Their green needles--like giant feather dusters--
Tickle the sky;
And the wind laughs.

Monster Love

Millie the monstrous
Led a sorrowful life.
All that she wanted
Was to be a good wife.

But who, pray tell,
Would a monstrous wed,
And take such a horrid
Creature to bed?

But, lo and alas,
It all came to pass,
For Millie the monstrous
Met a monster named Max.

To him she was lovely,
To her he was swell.
They married last week
At the bottom of the well.

Her life is now happy,
No more atrocities.
She plans to give birth
To baby monstrosities.

Donna A. Monday

Baby's First Haircut

I put him in his wagon
And pulled him to the shop,
And told the waiting barber,
"Just a little off the top."

He smiled at me as barbers smile
At anxious first-time mothers,
Who think that these are all life's curls,
That there will be no others.

But, understandably he cut
What he called an "angel trim,"
And left the shock above the eyes,
"Well-named," I said to him.

And so we left the barber shop
All strew with strawberry curl,
And he crawled into the wagon,
More boy, at last, than girl.

In the Garden

Timothy Turnip
Lives in the garden;
His roots are very deep.
His hair is red
And when he goes to bed
He sings himself to sleep.

Oliver Onion
Lives in the garden.
He's fluffy and green on top.
I still don't know why
He makes people cry,
But he simply can't seem to stop.

Christopher Cornstalk
Lives in the garden;
He's brown and a wee bit smug.
He's exceptionally tall,
And that's not all.
He has his own ladybug.

Petunia Potato
Lives in the garden.
She has an apartment below.
She's wobbly and round,
Weighs a quarter of a pound,
And rolls where she wants to go.

Donna A. Monday

Reginald Radish
Lives in the garden.
He wears a leafy hat.
His tummy's red,
And by all 'tis said
That Reggie is getting fat.

Now once a week,
When the farmer's asleep--
While the cow jumps over the moon--
These folks all meet on Huckle Street
To play a little tune.

They've formed a rock group
Called Vegetable Soup,
And they sing, they dance, and they sup.
Then a quick, "Beg your pardon,"
And it's back to the garden
Before the farmer gets up.

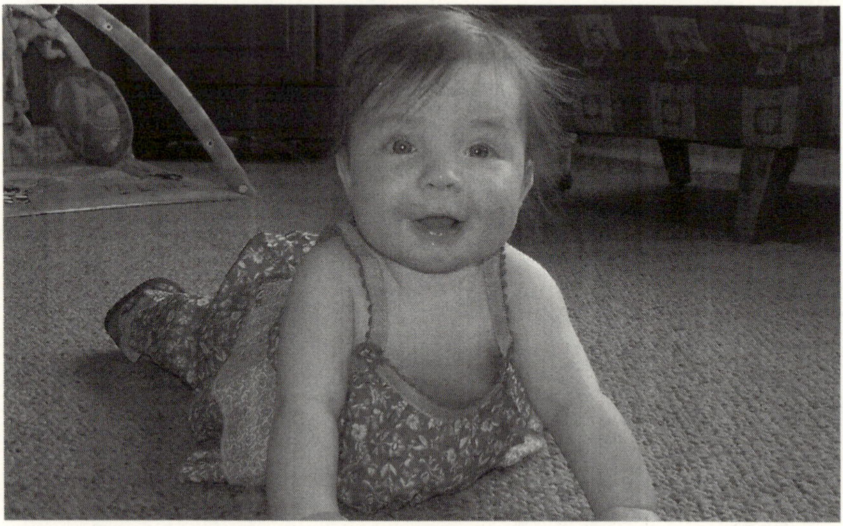

Baby's Day

Balloons, begonias, and bubble gum,
A fuzzy blanket,
A tasty thumb.
A horsey ride on Grandpa's knee,
A dandelion,
A honey bee.
A chocolate bar,
A teddy bear,
A story told
In a rocking chair.
A cuddly puppy,
A wagon ride,
A silly game
Of seek and hide.
A bubbly bath,
A brand new friend.
Oh, would this day
Would never end.

With Child

Man may plant the seed,
But he knows not the rest,
And in the months of knowing,
The woman is the blessed.

To a Newborn

When Mommy was expecting a baby,
And nobody knew just who,
All of us were secretly hoping
The baby would be you.

Happy "birth" day, Little One

Blow It

Charlie Barley has a cold;
His nose is always runny.
And every time he snuffs it up,
His mom says, "Blow it, Sonny."

The Clown

A polka-dotted clown
Came dancing into town
And did a beggar meet.
"Tell me," said the clown,
"Which way is down,"
And the beggar touched his feet.

Donna A. Monday

The Turtle

I found a little turtle.
It was underneath a shrub.
He was very, very dirty;
So I washed him in the tub.
I dried him with a towel
And put him on a chair;
But when my mother found him,
I wished he wasn't there.

Jennifer Johnson

Jennifer Johnson
Has a great big swing
That hangs from a great big tree;
And every day when we go out to play,
She tries to swing higher than me.

Jennifer Johnson
Has carrot red hair
And freckles all over her face;
And when we are swingin' and start in to singin'
She always loses her place.

Now, swingin' is easy
In a great big swing,
And singin' is easy, I guess.
But to swing while you sing is a much harder thing,
And Jennifer's simply a mess.

Tommy Turtle

Tiny Tommy Turtle
Simply could not find his shell;
So to the oyster's party
He had to wear a bell.

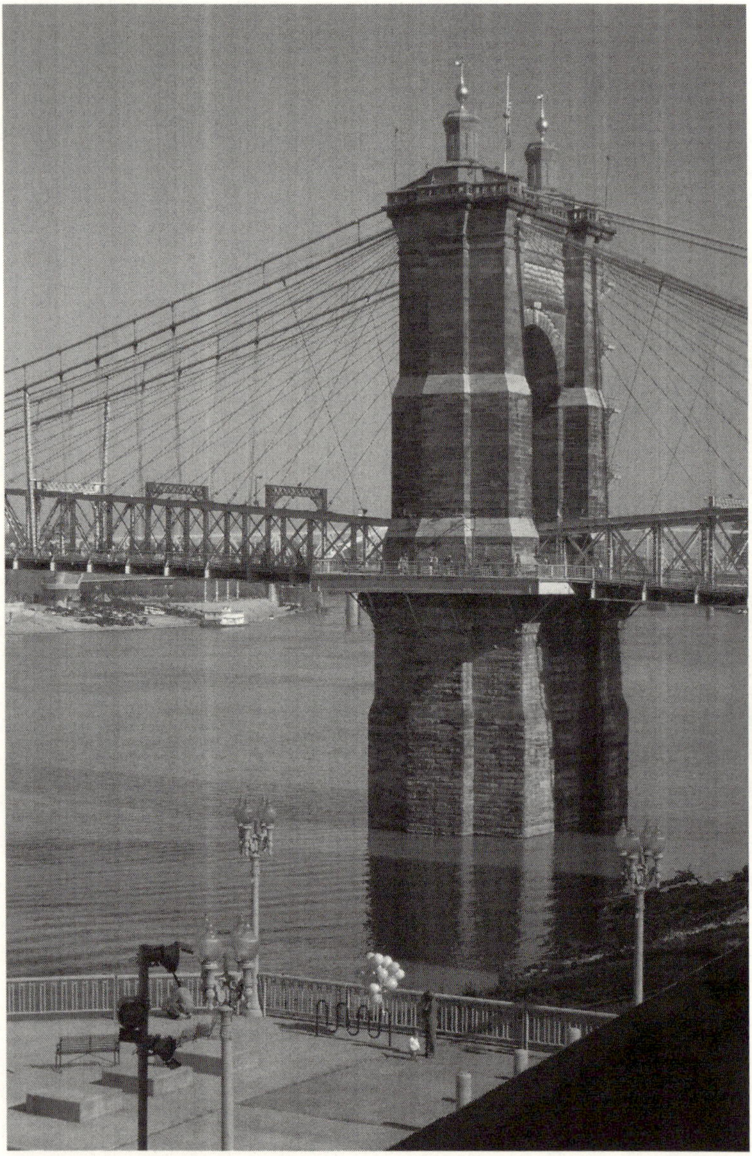

Playing

Charlie and April and Cathy and Bill
Are four little children
Who were playing on a hill.

Charlie said to Bill,
"There are monsters on the bridge.
"There are robbers on the highway;
"There are soldiers on the ridge."

April said to Cathy,
"Don't you listen to my brother.
"Before I get afraid of things,
"I'm gonna ask my mother."

Noises

What kind of noise
Do you like the best?
Squeaks, say I,
Beat all the rest.

Rattles are nice
And bangs okay,
But squeaks are the finest
Of noises today.

Moans are scary,
And screams are frightful;
But squeaks, I think,
Are just delightful.

Donna A. Monday

Puppy

I call my puppy Panda
Because he's black and white.
I could have called him Zebra,
But Panda sounded right.

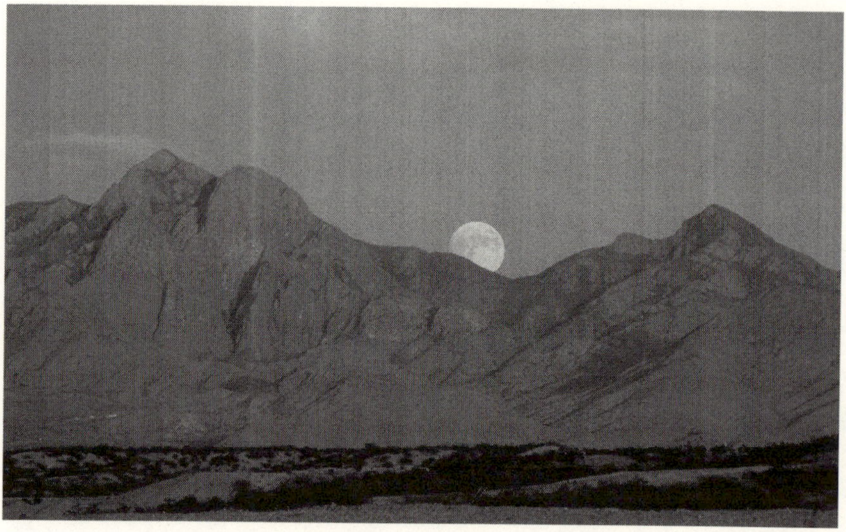

Night

The night train whistles
And its rumble breaks
The giant round silence
That the big moon makes.
Its rumble is a rattle--
Then a murmur--
Then it's gone;
And the giant round silence
Is quiet on a throne.

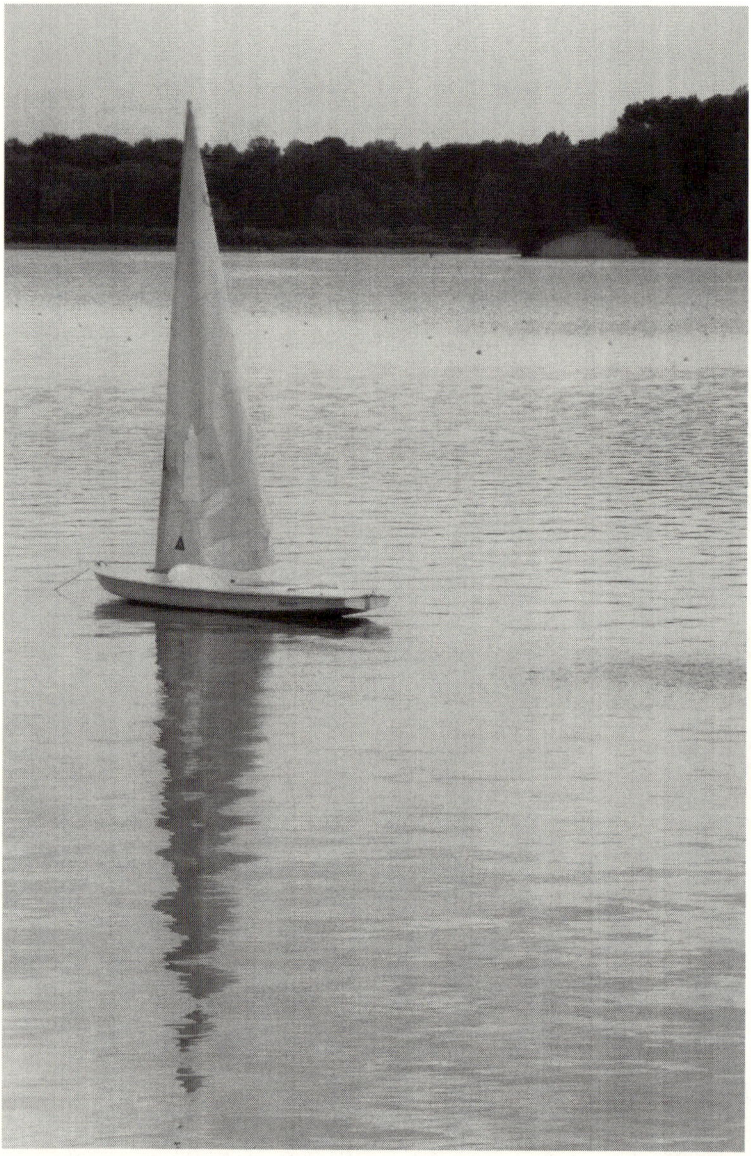

Sailing

Would you like to go a'sailing,
Just you and me and the sea,
With a blustering wind
And a thermos of tea,
And perhaps a box of Cracker Jacks?

No, let's forget the sailing,
And just sit here by the sea.
We'll munch our box of Cracker Jacks,
And sip our cups of tea,

While we watch the big boats race,
And the little fellows, too;
You root for the red one,
I'll root for the blue.

We'll sift the sand between our toes
And sniff the salty air.
We needn't really take a trip,
'Cause we're already there.

I'll let you kiss me on the lips
If you will hold my hand.
And when we grow up we'll be lovers,
Like the water and the sand.

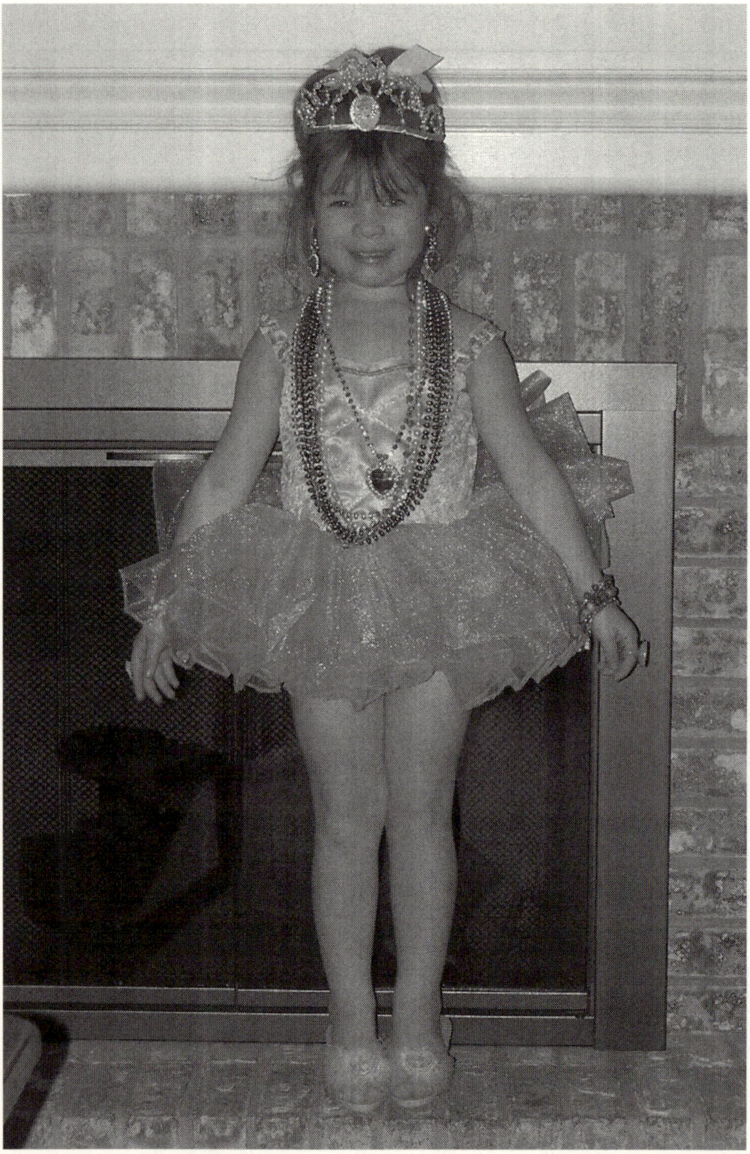

Just You Wait

I can roar; I can zoom.
I can clean up my room,
And say my letters from A to Z.

I can hide; I can wink.
I can say what I think.
I can hang by my knees from a tree.

I can skip; I can hop
And do a flip flop,
Or close my eyes and play dead.

I can run; I can jump
And land on my rump.
I can even stand on my head.

I can sing; I can shout.
I can let the dog out.
I can hold the door for my dad.

I can laugh; I can sneeze.
I can say "thank you" and "please."
I can be good; or I can be bad.

I can work; I can play.
I can sleep in all day.
I can dance on the kitchen floor.

And if you like me today,
Then all I can say,
Is just wait 'til next year when I'm four.

Air Mail to Santa Claus

I wanted to write a letter
To send to Mr. Claus,
But I didn't know exactly
What his North Pole address was.

So I stamped it with a pine cone.
I sealed it with some snow,
Then Tossed it to the wind
And let my letter blow.

Do you think he got it?

Donna A. Monday

I Wish I Was a Tiger

I wish I was a tiger
With fierce, strong jaws,
Stripes on my body,
And claws on my paws.

Eyes as bright as marbles,
Teeth as sharp as knives.
I wish I was a tiger,
And I had nine lives.

Ode to a Teddy Bear

You--the one on the middle shelf--
The one so smugly by yourself.
Who stitched that fuzzy little nose?
Who tacked those button eyes?
Who stuffed you in those silly clothes?
What makes you look so wise?
I like that patchwork shirt, you know;
It fits you to a tee.
Go fetch your price tag, Teddy Bear.
You're coming home with me.

Donna A. Monday

Mustn't Do

Some things are for picking--
Like daffodils and roses.
Other things are not--
Like ears, and teeth, and noses.

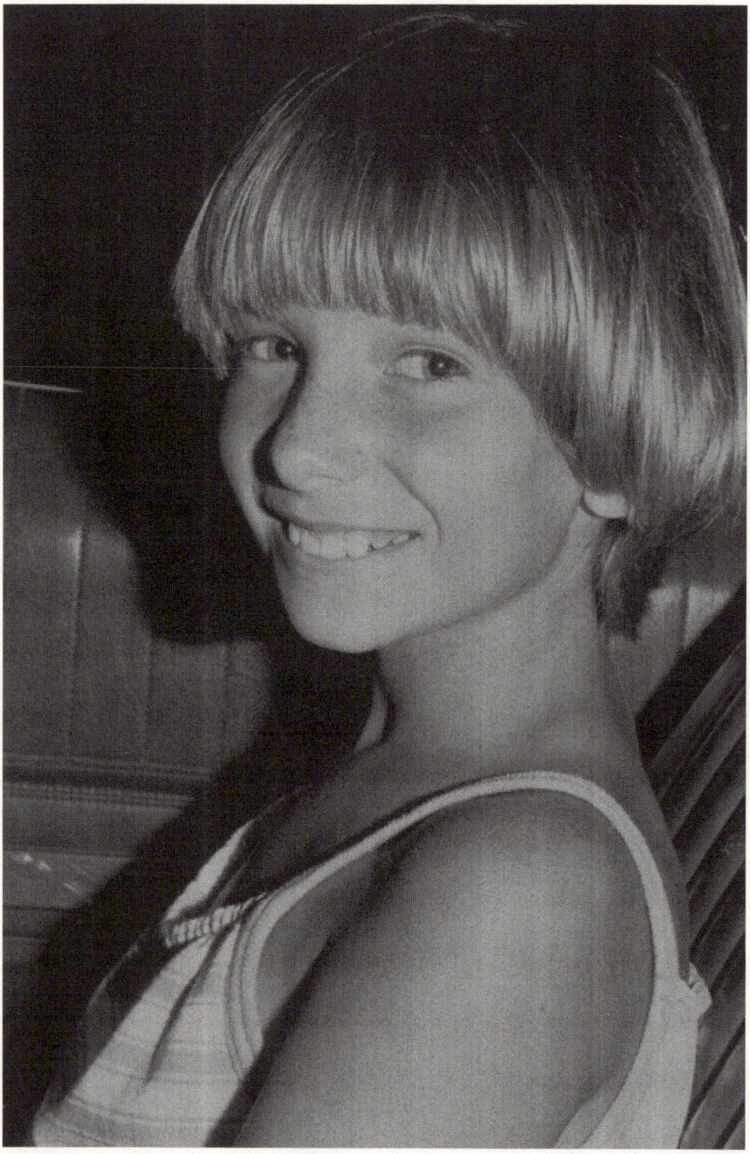

April Grows Up

(1st birthday)

April had a party,
With gifts and bows, and balloons
And chocolate cake with icing,
And little forks and spoons.

And hot dogs and potato chips
And orange juice in a cup,
And little friends and she sat down
And gobbled it all up.

Yes, April had a party,
And she wore a party dress,
And no cared for just this once
If April made a mess.

(at 12)

April is a dewdrop;
April is the rain.
April is the sunshine,
Fresh and new again.

April is a redbud,
A thick and luscious fog,
April is a violet
Underneath a log.

April is a promise;
April is a dawn.
April is assurance
The winter chill is gone.

April is illusion,
Her leaves are still but lace.
April is my daughter
And the love that lights her face.

(at graduation)

April as a maiden,
Is all I hoped she'd be,
She's fair of face,
A study in grace,
A joy for all to see.

She kept her sense of playfulness,
Her friendship and her fun.
She's added to that wisdom,
And now she's just begun...

A flower in the blooming,
A blossom in the sun.